Willow Finds ar

A Willow Codes adventure

WILLOW CODES

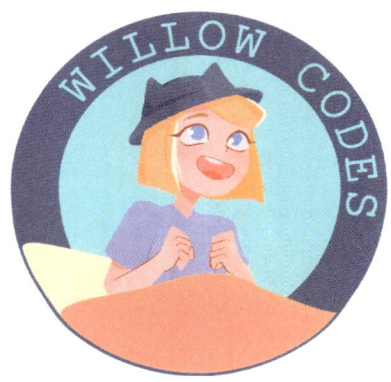

This book can be used alongside the programming language Scratch.

Scratch is a coding language and online community where you can create your own interactive stories, games, and animations -- and share your creations with others around the world. As young people create and share Scratch projects, they learn to think creatively, reason systematically, and work collaboratively.

Scratch is a project of the Scratch Foundation in collaboration with the Lifelong Kindergarten group at the MIT Media Lab. It is available for free at https://scratch.mit.edu

Copyright year: 2021
Copyright Notice: by Rebecca Franks. All rights reserved.
The above information forms this copyright notice: © 2021 by Rebecca Franks. All rights reserved.

This book is dedicated to
Annalyn, Hayden and Beatrice

Willow hated tidying her bedroom. Thankfully, she had a great way of making boring things fun.

Willow's dress up box helped her be whoever and wherever she wanted.

Today, she would be an explorer!

"Hopper, can you reach up and put those pieces in their places, please?"

Hopper got to work on following the instructions.

"Oh no!" Willow realized. "You need precise instructions. I forgot."

"Hopper...followed...instructions..."

"Don't worry Hopper, we can try again," explained Willow.

"Hopper, pick up the yellow circle and place it in the circle hole."

"Hopper, pick up the orange triangle and place it in the triangle hole."

"Hopper, pick up the blue square and place it in the square hole."

"Yay! We did it!" Willow cheered.

Willow's Mum called from downstairs, "Willow! You have thirty minutes to get that bedroom tidy!"

"Quick Hopper, we need to hurry!"

Hopper had some handy blocks of code to help Willow.

"You can use...these blocks... to give me some precise... instructions...for the next... puzzle."

Hopper continued, "Make sure...to place them... in the correct...order.

Press my green flag... when you are ready...to try out...the code blocks."

"Okay!" Willow agreed. "I will try your code."

Willow placed the blocks in order.

Willow jumps for joy. "Wow, I'm finally getting the hang of this!"

"Willow! You have ten minutes left!" Mum called from downstairs. "Make sure you don't forget about that egg!"

"Oh wow! This looks like a tricky maze! It looks like I need to collect all of the socks before reaching the egg." Willow explained.

"I have new blocks...for you. These are subroutines...that you can call...to get me to follow a specific sequence."

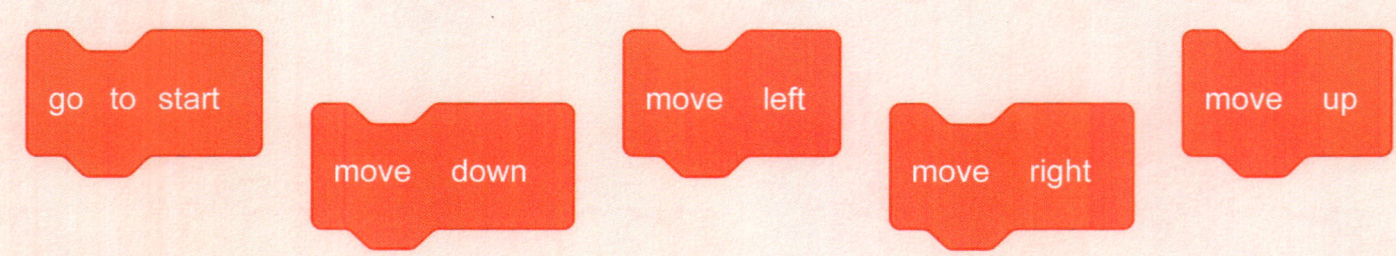

"You can use them...as many times...as you need... and in any order...press my green flag...when you are ready."

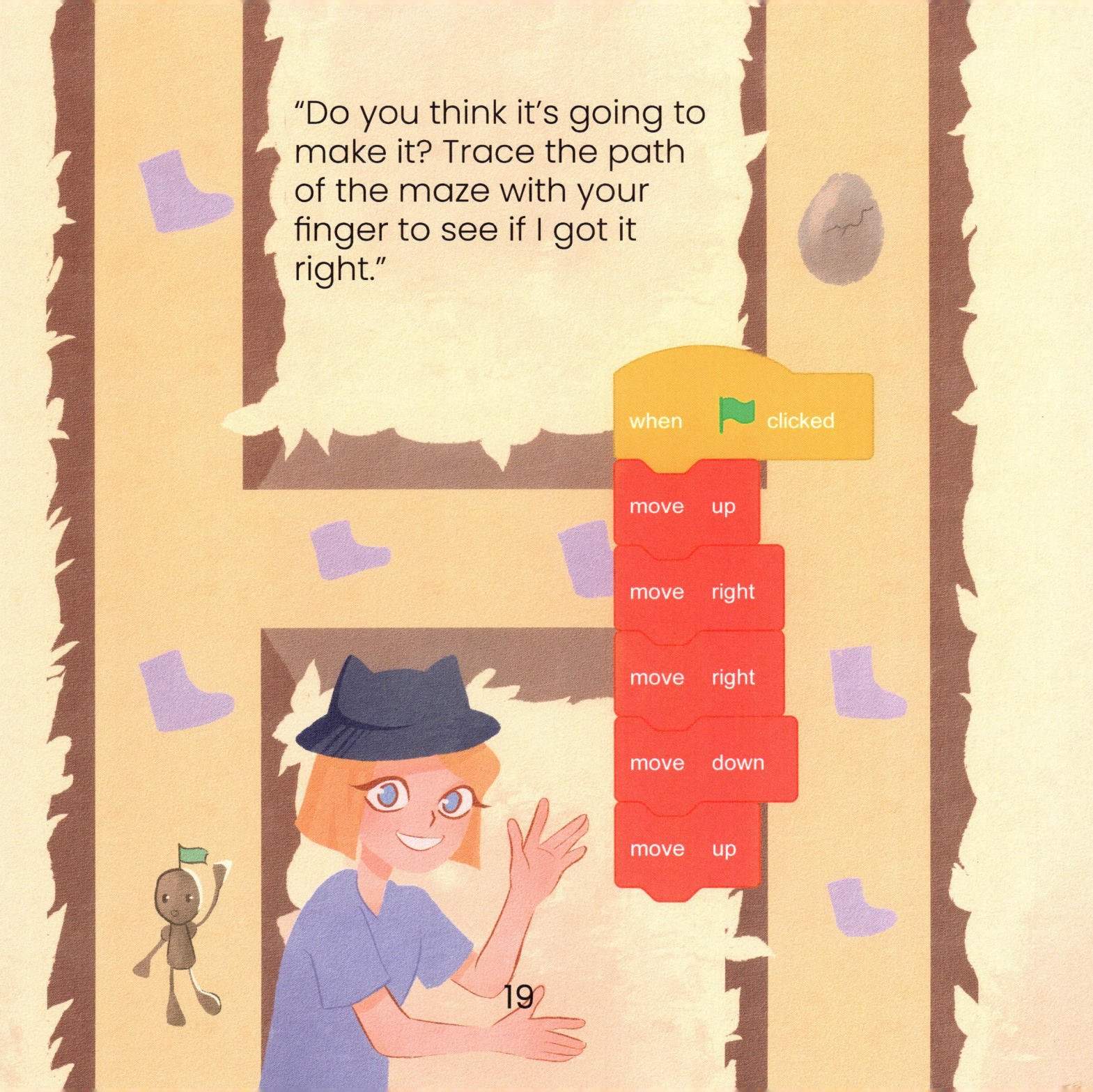

"What do you think? Is it going to work this time? Trace the path with your finger to see if it works."

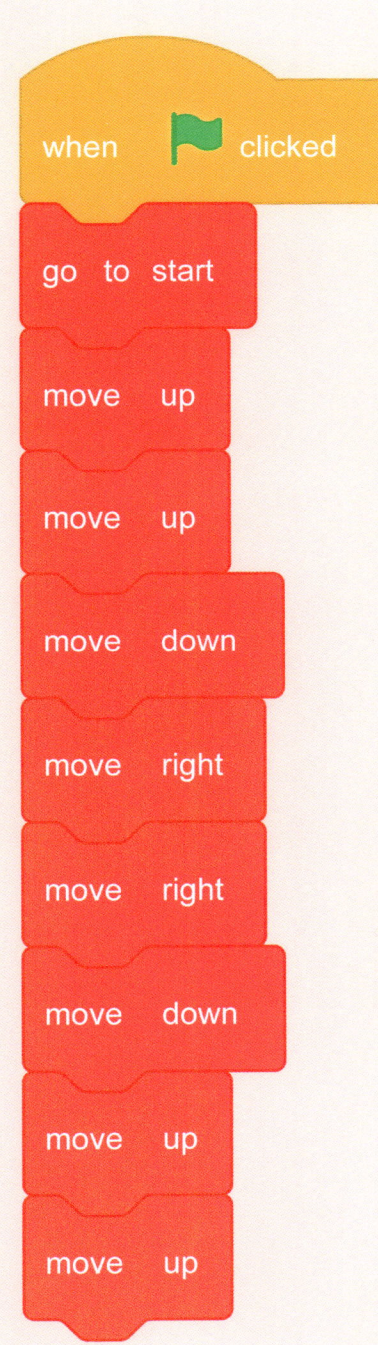

"What do you think? Did I get it right this time?"

"I will call you pixel!"

"I am very impressed. You cleaned your room very well!" Mum said. "I see you also found the egg. I love your new pet!"

"Here is your tablet. What are you going to do with it today?" Mum asked.

"Oh, I think I will try some coding!"

Do you want to try coding like Willow?

Visit **willowcodes.com** to get started!

willowcodes.com

Printed in Great Britain
by Amazon